My Name on the Wind

THE LOCKERT LIBRARY
OF POETRY IN TRANSLATION

For other titles in the Lockert Library see page 141

My Name on the Wind

Selected Poems of Diego Valeri

Translated by Michael Palma

PRINCETON UNIVERSITY PRESS

Copyright © 1989 by Princeton University Press

Published by Princeton University Press,
41 William Street, Princeton,
New Jersey 08540

In the United Kingdom: Princeton University
Press, Guildford, Surrey

All Rights Reserved

The Lockert Library of Poetry in Translation
is supported by a bequest from
Charles Lacy Lockert (1888-1974)

This book has been composed in Linotron
Palatino type

Clothbound editions of Princeton University Press
books are printed on acid-free paper,
and binding materials are chosen for strength
and durability. Paperbacks, although satisfactory
for personal collections, are not usually
suitable for library rebinding.

Printed in the United States of America
by Princeton University Press,
Princeton, New Jersey

Library of Congress
Cataloging-in-Publication Data

Valeri, Diego, 1887-1976.
My name on the wind : selected poems of Diego
Valeri / translated by Michael Palma.
p.   cm.—(Lockert library of poetry in translation)
ISBN 0-691-06776-7 ISBN 0-691-01462-0 (pbk.)
1. Valeri, Diego, 1887-1976—Translations, English.
I. Palma, Michael, 1945-   . II. Title. III. Series.
PQ4847.A44A26 1989
851'.912—dc19   88-27565

for Victoria

Contents

Preface	ix
Acknowledgments	xiii

From *Poesie* (1962; 1967)

1910–1930

Leaves, Falling Leaves . . .	5
Vicenza 1915	7
Spring in Ravenna	9
Those Mornings Long Ago	17
Evening in the Mountains	19
Window	21
Sister Gesuina	23
Sunday	27

1930–1950

Sunrise	31
Winter Song	33
Scirocco	35
Anacreontic	37
Portrait	39
Flower of Nothingness	41
Autumnal	43
The Vineyard	47
Dark Olive Trees	49
Spring	51
On the Shore of Sleep	53
Sea	55
Exile Camp	57

1950–1965: I

Waking	65
In Passing	67
Blade of Wind	69
The Air Still Chilly	71

1950–1965: II

Summer Sky	75

Solitude	77
Watercolor	79
Roman Summer	81
Remembrance of Gallipoli	83

From *Verità di uno* (1970)

Mythology	87
To Domenico Cantatore	89
One Day, Perhaps, This Way . . .	91
The Fig Tree	93

From *Calle del vento* (1975)

"Here there's always a bit of wind"	97
"Under the tree, here"	99
"Evening spreads across the sky"	101
"Back when I was a boy"	103
"Saba, Stuparich, Giotti"	105
"Springtime tender and unripe"	107
"Now you have gone away, leaving behind"	109
"The movement of the sun across our rooms"	111
"Fine sunlight spreads evenly"	113
"Once long ago under a hellish sky"	115
"That old old story"	117
"We make our way along the thread of years"	119
"The days, the months, the years"	121

From *Poesie inedite, o "come"* (1977)

"In Venice, as it rests upon its bed"	125
"And so I stopped"	127
"You who have eyes to witness miracles"	129
"With the look upon your face"	131

From *Tempo e Poesia* (1964)

The Old Poet and His Book	135

Preface

For whatever reasons, the Italian poets are even less well known to Americans than the poets of other European nations. I recall the Romantic poetry professor who cited to the class the names of Wordsworth's French and German contemporaries and concluded that "the Italians probably have their own Romantic poet"; I recall the friend, a widely read man who would have no trouble identifying Apollinaire or Mayakovsky, who read the introduction to my Gozzano translation and said, "In the first paragraph you mention this Ungaretti as if I should recognize the name." And yet even among many of those conversant with Leopardi, those for whom the name Quasimodo carries associations other than Charles Laughton, Diego Valeri remains obscure.

Given the bases of most international literary reputations, Valeri's lack of currency in this country is hardly surprising. In the early 1960s, in his mid-seventies, Valeri read the proofs of his collected poems. According to his essay "The Old Poet and His Book" (included in this volume), he reminisced, fretted, wondered whether his work had any value, and ultimately consoled himself that "in my book there is no pose, there is no trickery, there is no conformity, there is no anticonformity, there is no ideological enthusiasm for any party or point of view, there is no modish experimentalism, there is no lying of any kind, either moral or artistic." This statement proceeds from what Valeri elsewhere in the essay characterizes as a mixture of modesty (note that he concentrates exclusively on what his poetry does not contain) and "Luciferian pride."

His claim is fully justified, and his ability to make it is all the more remarkable in light of both the length of his life and career and the extent of his poetic output. Born in Piove di Sacco, near Padua, on January 25, 1887, Valeri lived to within two months of his ninetieth birthday, dying at his daughter's house in Rome on November 27, 1976. He took a degree in literature at the University of Padua in 1908 and pursued graduate studies at the Sorbonne in 1912 and 1913. After some years spent teaching in schools, he became a professor of modern French literature at the University of Padua, where he also taught modern and contemporary Italian literature. Beginning with *Le gaie tristezze* in 1913, he published nearly twenty volumes of poetry, as well as a considerable number of prose works: descriptions of his adopted and much-loved Venice, literary monographs, essays on art and artists (in 1967 appeared *Amico dei pittori*, a booklet of poems written in response to paintings by such artists as Carlo Carrà and Domenico Cantatore). Valeri also published a number of translations, including one of *Madame Bovary*, as well as selections from the fables of La Fontaine and the poetry of Goethe. His volume of collected poems (1962, augmented edition 1967) contains nearly two hundred Italian poems—and thirty in French—and he says that "I have sacrificed almost as many as I have saved." In his immensely productive last decade, he published yet another hundred poems.

The only directly positive claims provoked by his confrontation of the vast mass of his poetry are for a unified tone and sensibility and for simplicity and directness. Allowing for inevitable changes and developments in a career spanning two-thirds of a century (the later poems are invariably quite brief and generally much less formally strict), this claim too is largely justified. The title of the first collection provides an apt keynote not only in its paradox but even in its syntax: though the poems are modified by gaiety, it is the sadnesses that are substantive. Everywhere in Valeri's poetry the style is vivid, precise, and direct, the fittest instrument for a poet whose desire is to set down without pretense what he saw and what he felt. The risks in such an approach are obvious, and Valeri does not always escape them: many poems remain mere evocations of a landscape or a mood, inert and untransfigured. But in his best work there is not only a clarity of vision and a purity of style but a haunting and intense beauty. His immediacy seems at odds with the reflective mode of his Romantic inheritance (throughout his poetry, amid more complex treatments, appear a number of brief imagistic pieces that would have satisfied T. E. Hulme), and yet it is the poet's imagination that gives enduring life to the scenes and the events that have stimulated him. This point is suggested in the last stanza of "September Morning," a poem not otherwise noteworthy, in which the speaker describes a day spent with his young daughter:

> It was a September morning in a wood.
> Or perhaps I merely dreamt it, after all.
> If it was real, the day is long since dead,
> but if a dream, a dream still beautiful.

Valeri's poetry is unified thematically, from first to last, by his great love of nature, which he presents not only as beautiful but as sensuous and even sensual. Concurrent with this theme, and often intertwined with it, is his other great subject, an appreciation of the beauty and the love of women. Though the first-person pronoun abounds in his work, the speaker in these poems is largely without background, without attributes. Not until very late in his career does his poetry take an overtly autobiographical turn, with several charming childhood reminiscences, as well as a brief but moving poem on the death of his wife. Unusual, in the earlier work, for the directness of its inspiration is "Exile Camp." After the fall of Mussolini on July 25, 1943, Valeri became editor of the Venetian daily *Il Gazzetino* (his academic career had been suspended because of his opposition to the regime): on September 8, 1943, he was condemned for anti-Fascist activities by a Nazi-backed Special Tribunal and was forced to flee to a refugee camp in Switzerland for the duration of the war.

The integrity of the man informs the body of his poetry. That poetry was widely admired in his lifetime, and toward the end of his life he was the recipient of a number of literary awards in Italy and elsewhere in Europe. In the decade or so since his death, his poetry has held its place. Solidly constructed, sensitively written, deeply felt, it is animated by that impulse described by Robert Bridges:

> I love all beauteous things,
>   I seek and adore them;
> God hath no better praise,
> And man in his hasty days
>   Is honoured for them.
>
> I too will something make
>   And joy in the making;
> Altho' to-morrow it seem
> Like the empty words of a dream
>   Remembered on waking.

My chief criterion in this selection has, of course, been the quality of the individual poems. I have also sought to represent the range of Valeri's achievement, including several of his (relatively) longer poems and sequences, and including also several poems of an uncharacteristic but quite forceful harshness of tone and feeling. But perhaps most of all I have tried to catch and to communicate that "joy in the making" of even the bitterest or the saddest of these poems, that joy which is one of the infallible marks of the genuine poet.

Acknowledgments

I wish to thank Arnoldo Mondadori Editore (and especially Terri L. Feld of Mondadori's New York office) for its generous permission to reprint and to translate Valeri's work; Giorgio and Liliana DeVoto of Edizioni San Marco dei Giustiniani for the poems from *Poesie inedite o "come"*; and New Rivers Press for permission to reprint "The Days, the Months, the Years," which appeared in the anthology *Poems from Italy*, edited by William Jay Smith and Dana Gioia. Marina Valeri Garretto and Giovanna Valeri De Santis, the poet's daughters, replied most graciously and helpfully to my letters; the opportunity to correspond with them was an unexpected and profound pleasure. Signora Garretto in particular was of invaluable assistance in providing information and securing permissions. Several friends read certain of these translations and made excellent suggestions for improvement: Peter Chetta, Dana Gioia, Robert Monteleone, Thomas Pendleton, and Cedric Winslow. Robert E. Brown more than confirmed my previous experience of the friendly and generous spirit of the Princeton University Press; and I am grateful to Catherine Thatcher not only for the unerring skill and exemplary tact of her editing but also for her friendship. My greatest debt, an incalculable one, is to Victoria Coughlin, for responding to these poems with sensitivity and insight, for prodding me to finish and to submit the manuscript, and for loving both Valeri and his translator.

From *Poesie* (1962; 1967)

1910-1930

Foglie, giú foglie . . .

Foglie, giú foglie nella lenta pioggia
di questa dolce disperata sera!
Foglie, giú foglie: grandi pese fracide
foglie d'ippocastano, e verdi e lievi
e trepide fogliette di robinia;
giú, per l'albore freddo dei lampioni,
giú, sul lucido asfalto della via . . .

E noi due si cammina si cammina,
senza parlare, l'uno accanto all'altra,
portando in cuore faticosamente
la stessa soma di malinconia.

Foglie, giú foglie. E c'è forse qualcosa
che muore intanto nella nostra vita,
che cosí muore, e non vuole morire.

Leaves, Falling Leaves . . .

Leaves, falling leaves in the softly falling rain,
coming down on this sweet evening of despair.
Leaves, falling leaves, great heavy soaking wet
leaves from the chestnut tree, and light and green
and trembling little leaves from the locust tree,
down through the chilly brightness of the lamplight,
down on the glossy asphalt of the street . . .

And here the two of us are walking, walking,
without a word, the one beside the other,
each carrying the burden of the same
full weight of melancholy in the heart.

Leaves, falling leaves. Between us there may be
something that dies in the middle of our life,
that dies this way, and doesn't want to die.

Vicenza 1915

Grigiori d'alba. Nella muta via
che sa di pane fresco e di rugiada
scoppia improvviso un tuono di fanfara:
il battaglione alpino se ne va . . .

Imposte sbatacchiate. Alle finestre,
donne in camicia tra gerani in fiore.
E un bandierone di vento e di sole
d'un tratto avvolge tutta la città.

Vicenza 1915

Gray of daybreak. Into the silent street
fragrant with fresh bread and dew there comes
a sudden blare of bugles and of drums:
the alpine battalion's ready to march on . . .

Slapping of shutters. Women in nightgowns
framed in the windows amid geraniums.
And then the entire city all at once
is wrapped in a huge flag of wind and sun.

Primavera di Ravenna

Dentro una vasta nuvola rosata
Aprile è giunto per le vie dell'aria
su la città che cova solitaria
il suo vecchio dolor di spodestata,

e di là è sceso sovra l'ali aperte
a spandere le sue consolazioni
sui viali romito dei bastioni
e su le piazze pallide e deserte.

Poi col suo passo morbido di vento
s'è addentrato pei vicoli contorti,
pei cupi androni e nei chiassuoli morti,
alle cose piú tristi sorridendo . . .

Ha la sua gemma adesso ogni finestra:
un rubino, un topazio, una turchese;
la piú povera e sola delle chiese
adesso ha il paramento della festa;

l'erba del ciottolato è un tremolio
di luce d'oro, il musco dei gradini
è un velluto dai lampi smeraldini,
il rigagnolo un bianco luccichio . . .

Si; ma nel fondo il cuor non è mutato:
chi sta, la sera, con gli orecchi intenti
ode le vecchie pietre sofferenti
piangere un lento pianto soffocato;

chi guarda attorno nella notte scura
vede dall'ombra mute larve uscire
e nell'ombra fuggevoli svanire,
con occhi folli d'odio e di paura . . .

Spring in Ravenna

Now April has arrived within a vast
rose-colored cloud along the airy roads
above the city (city that sits and broods
over its ancient pain of the dispossessed),

and spilling her consolations everywhere,
upon her outspread wings she has descended
on the hermetic avenues defended
with bastions, and the pale deserted squares.

Then, on the tender footsteps of the wind
she reaches into twisting alleyways,
into the dead ends and dark passages,
smiling upon the sad things of the land . . .

Now every window has its own display,
a ruby or a turquoise or topaz.
Now even the poorest of the churches has
the festive trappings of a holiday.

The gutter is a glistening of white,
the moss upon the steps an emerald green
flashing of velvet, and the grass between
the cobblestones a trembling of gold light . . .

The heart's depths are untouched by the bright tones.
Whoever stands and listens now, with ears
intent upon the gathered evening, hears
the slow and smothered tears of the old stones.

Whoever peers into the murky night
sees phantoms scurry from the shadows, then
slip back into the shadows once again,
their mad eyes filled with hatred and with fright . . .

Per sapere la gioia dell'aprile
bisogna, amici, uscir per i sobborghi,
mirare il ciel le vie dorate e gli orti,
e i colli che traspaiono laggiú.

Serenità divina: azzurro e azzurro.
I carrettieri passano cantando;
si rincorrono i bimbi strepitando;
stan su l'uscio le donne a comarò.

Una gallina ci attraversa il passo
e becca ai nostri piedi un verme rosso;
gli anitroccoli biondi accanto al fosso
si spulciano con gaia alacrità . . .

Prime foglie tremanti su la rama
nuda, o lucenti nella terra bruna!
Si vorrebbe baciarle ad una ad una,
piangendo di dolcezza e di bontà.

Ecco un pèsco fiorito, piú soave
di soave fanciulla adolescente,
ecco un ciliegio piú forte e splendente
dell'uomo arriso dalla gioventú.

Una distesa d'orti. In primo piano:
selvette d'insalata ricciolina,
viali d'aglio, qualche testolina
di fagiolo che spunta a far cucú;

dietro: tappeti di varia verdura
distesi in simmetria, tende pezzate,
molli trapunte scure fiocchettate
di verze gialle e cavolfiori blu;

To know the joy of April, you must go,
my friends, out to the suburbs: you must know
the golden roads, the yards where gardens grow,
the hills that shine beneath wide skies of blue.

Blue, endless blue: divine serenity.
The wagon drivers singing as they pass,
the shouting children chasing through the grass,
the women in the doorways gossiping.

A hen comes clucking right across our path;
between our feet she pecks at a red worm.
Beside the ditch the yellow ducklings swarm
and pick at themselves with gay alacrity . . .

The first leaves trembling on the naked branch,
bright points on the brown land that's still asleep.
You long to kiss them one by one, and weep
with sweetness and with generosity.

Here is a blooming peach tree, softer than
an adolescent girl so soft and tender,
and here a cherry tree stronger in its splendor
than a man that youth gives all her bounty to.

Fields of unfolding gardens. Near at hand:
a thicket full of richly curling greens,
long rows of garlic, here and there some beans
whose tips are sprouting, playing peekaboo.

On the other side: the stretching symmetries
of dappled awnings, carpets every shade
of green, and soft dark quilts with tassels made
of yellow cabbage, cauliflower of blue.

nello sfondo: robinie che la guazza
ha ingioiellato di puri diamanti,
un filare di pioppi palpitanti . . .
e il cielo azzurro . . . la serenità . . .

Si va col passo dei conquistatori,
col cuore acceso nell'aperta mano.
Vogliam gettarlo, amici, al ciel lontano,
o al balcone che primo s'aprirà?

. . . Ma in questo pomeriggio veneziano
tutto languori ed iridi d'opale
andremo a passeggiar, pensando il mare,
per l'argine solingo del Candiano.

Giaccion dieci paranze e un vaporino
nell'acque cupe e viscide del porto,
tra il sudiciume d'un binario morto
e lo squallor d'un chiuso magazzino.

Stinte le chiglie, verdi rosse e nere,
screpolata la pelle di catrame,
nuda la nervatura del cordame;
povere barche morte prigioniere!

Ma che gioia, alla svolta! È un palpitare
vasto d'azzurro tra una rosea bruma,
con indolenze grigie di laguna
e verdissimi brividi di mare . . .

Off in the distance: locust trees bejewelled
with purest diamonds by the morning dew,
a row of throbbing poplars . . . skies of blue . .
and everywhere a deep serenity . . .

You walk that country like a conqueror,
and hold in your open hand a heart on fire.
Friends, shall we toss it toward the distant sky,
or onto the first opened balcony?

. . . But in this languorous, Venetian-style
afternoon of iridescent opal air,
all thinking of the sea, we walk the bare
embankment of the Candiano Canal.

Ten trawlers and a steamboat lie at rest
in the dark and slimy waters of the harbor,
between a railroad siding strewn with garbage
and an empty warehouse sunk in dreariness.

The faded keels once green and black and red,
tar caulking with its chapped and cracking skin,
exposed nerves of the rigging frayed and thin:
poor boats made prisoners and left for dead.

Around the bend, pure joy—an immensity
of living blue between the mists of rose,
here the lagoon in lazy gray repose
and there the deep green shivering of the sea.

Voi mi parlate, amici, ed io non v'odo,
mentre vi seguo per la bianca via,
poi che il dolce velen di nostalgia
m'ha inebriato il cuore; e soffro e godo . .

Un'altra svolta, ed ecco s'allontana,
si spalanca e s'abbassa l'orizzonte.
Un infinito di brughiere bionde.
E nel silenzio . . . s'ode il mar che chiama

No, non è il mar che chiama: è la pineta
che tutta trema sotto la carezza
lenta e profonda della calda brezza,
e ride e geme con ansia segreta.

Ella si sta su l'altra riva, stesa
supina, molle, pallido rosata,
come un'amante stanca e non saziata,
che teme e chiede la soave offesa . . .

O carnali blandizie dell'aprile!
Quest'aria, amici, quest'odor di mare,
questo cielo, m'han fatto ubriacare . . .
Riducetemi voi nel queto ovile.

You speak to me, but I don't hear, my friends.
I follow you along the sunbleached road.
The poison of nostalgia's overflowed
my drunken heart: it exults and it laments . . .

Another bend: in the distance suddenly
wide vistas sloping down to the horizon.
An infinity of yellow heaths. And silence . . .
And now we hear the beckoning of the sea.

No, it's not the sea that's calling. It's the pines,
the forest trembling in the deep caress
of the warm, slow breeze. It laughs in restlessness,
and in its secret urgency it moans.

Supine and soft, with its pale rosy tints,
it stretches before us on the other side,
like a mistress tired and unsatisfied
who dreads and craves the exquisite offense.

By April's carnal blandishments cajoled—
the air, my friends, the fragrance of the sea,
the sky—they've all intoxicated me . . .
You drive me back into the docile fold.

I mattini d'allora

I mattini d'allora . . . Portavano negli occhi
una profonda luce immacolata,
un fresco fiore di desiderio in bocca,
nelle mani una piccola gioia inaspettata.

I mattini d'allora . . . Ci chiamavano per nome,
ch'era tempo di ridere, di cantare, d'amare.
L'amico correva all'amico, a rinnovare
il patto di fraterna comunione.

I mattini d'allora . . . Ci venivano incontro
per le pallide vie della piccola città
col passo molle e baldo delle giovani donne
calde di sconosciute voluttà.

I mattini d'allora . . . Ci traevano incantati
a veder le robinie piegate dalla rugiada,
i giaggioli d'oro su le prode dei fossati,
le mille meraviglie della strada.

I mattini d'allora . . . d'allora! Il nostro cuore
era semplice e buono e senza ferita.
Un'amata ci dava tutto il suo amore:
la vita.

Those Mornings Long Ago

Those mornings long ago . . . They brought, each day,
eyes shining with a clear and steady fire,
hands filled with some small unexpected joy,
a mouth with the fresh flower of desire.

Those mornings long ago . . . They called to us
by name, as friend went hurrying after friend,
joined in a pact of brotherhood. It was
a time of song, of love and laughter, then.

Those mornings long ago . . . They arrived upon
young women's footsteps: boldly and delicately
they walked in the pale streets of the little town,
flushed with their buried sensuality.

Those mornings long ago . . . They gently drew
our eyes to where the golden iris glowed
by the ditch's edge, to the locust bent with dew,
to the thousand miracles along the road.

Those mornings long ago . . . so long ago!
Our simple hearts had yet to know the knife.
We had a mistress then who loved us so:
life.

Sera tra i monti

L'aria non ha piú colore.
Il cielo, sopra le vette,
dure pallide nette,
s'illanguidisce e si sfa.

L'acqua non ha piú splendore.
Sopra il cristallo del lago
è un muto transcorrere vago
di tremule oscurità.

La terra ha chiuso il suo cuore.
I neri boschi d'abeti,
confusi opachi quieti,
non hanno palpito piú.

Tu, anima, apri il tuo fiore
piccolo, di luce infinita.
Anche una stella è fiorita,
piccola e infinita, lassú.

Evening in the Mountains

Air is paler than before.
The peaks are clear and high;
above the peaks the sky
starts to weaken and to fade.

The water dims once more.
The long light softly shakes
above the crystal lakes
and folds into the shade.

The earth seals up its core.
In forests dense with firs
dark and solid, nothing stirs
as blurring shadows fall.

You, spirit, open your
small flower of infinite light.
One star in the far night
flowers, infinite and small.

Vetrata

Fermo sopra la valle ottenebrata,
tra il rabesco della ramaglia nera,
il tramonto invernale
s'ergeva in fiamme, come una vetrata
di cattedrale.

Window

Motionless over the valley thick with shadow,
framed in the arabesque of the black branches,
in winter at nightfall
the sunset was aflame, like a stained-glass window
in a cathedral.

Suor Gesuina

Quando l'alba, cosí pura e mesta,
vaporò da quei tetti di rosa,
non so che soavità angosciosa
mi venne al cuore, dalla finestra.

C'era un piare d'uccello solo;
poi scoppiarono gli aspri gridi
delle rondini, sbucate dai nidi,
rovesciate nella furia del volo.

Tacquero a un tratto gli ululati
di quel povero moribondo,
e salí da un cortile profondo
la preghiera dei bimbi malati.

(Quella preghiera, a coro, sommessa,
tu l'hai ascoltata, anima sorda;
l'hai ricevuta, anima lorda,
come un'assoluzione promessa.)

E fu il giorno. E vidi apparire
al mio letto suor Gesuina
con la sua carità di morfina,
angelo nero del dolce morire.

Voci vicine, udite lontane;
uno scalpíccio di spettri bianchi
sgusciati fuori dai muri bianchi,
tra un tumulto di bianche campane.

Sister Gesuina

As the dawn mists began to depart
from the pink roofs mournfully,
came a strange tender misery
through the window into my heart.

A lone bird was chirping nearby.
Then the swallows with raucous bursts
came swarming up from their nests
and hurled themselves into the sky.

From below in the deep courtyard,
as the half-dead wretch near me
ceased his moaning suddenly,
rose a prayer from the children's ward.

(That soft chorused supplication,
you hearkened to it, deaf soul.
You felt it in your stained soul
as a promise of absolution.)

It was day. And beside my bed
appeared Sister Gesuina
with her charity of morphine,
a black angel of sweet death.

In a riot of white bells,
near voices, heard from afar.
Shuffling white phantoms appear
and slip beyond the white walls.

E corridoi. Senza fine andare
sul carrello cigolante;
e la testa cosí pesante
non poterla un poco levare.

Ma poi la mite benda su gli occhi;
su le labbra la ventosa verde
dell'etere. Il mio corpo si perde
come nuvola che si sfiocchi.

La morte (brancico ancóra ostinato
dietro un pensiero) la morte non duole.
E piú nulla. Un gorgo di sole
tenebroso m'ha inabissato.

Aperti gli occhi, rividi le rose
sotto il quadro della Madonna,
e la tenda nel sole bionda,
e il cielo, e gli uomini, e le cose . . .

Come stanco mi sentii il cuore,
ritornato dal nero esiglio
—senza un conforto, senza un consiglio—
alla sua sorte di dolore:

ansia d'amore, atroce male
di far soffrire, folle bisogno
di possedere in un sogno di sogno
tutta la bellezza mortale . . .

Venne allora suor Gesuina,
portando sul distrutto viso
un'umile carità di sorriso;
e parve la Misericordia divina.

A stretcher, a rattling ride
down the corridors' twisting ways,
a head too heavy to raise
or move from side to side.

On the eyes a soft white shroud,
the green ether cone at the lips,
and the body slowly slips
away, like a melting cloud . . .

Death, death (I tenaciously grope
for a thought) it's not painful at all.
Toward a vortex of dark sun I fall,
it opens and swallows me up.

Eyes opened, I saw once again
the roses in front of the Virgin's
picture, the pale sunlit curtains,
the sky, and the things, and the men . .

My heart ached with weariness,
brought back from the dark and the cold
uncounseled and unconsoled
to its destiny of distress:

the fever of love, foul desires
to spread suffering, the mad gleam
to possess in the dream of a dream
all that is lovely and dies . . .

Then came Sister Gesuina to me
with her face so worn and ancient:
I could dream of divine compassion
in her smile's humble charity.

Domenica

Piú campane, in un'aria piú vuota.
Voci rade su lunghi susurri.
Entra per i finestroni azzurri
la domenica triste e devota.

I malati si guardan le mani,
giallastre sul lenzuolo bianco:
odono salire dal cuore stanco
sperduti echi d'anni lontani . . .

Ora, la domenica d'ospedale,
in cuffia bianca e veste nera,
s'aggira dicendo la sua preghiera
per il vuoto bianco delle sale.

Il vecchio non vede, non sente:
supino nel suo lettuccio, immoto,
tiene fisse su un altro vuoto
le grandi pupille spente.

Súbito scattano, da dietro
i tetti, le rondini, a colpo di vento,
e tagliano il cielo, stridendo
come il diamante sul vetro.

Sunday

Bells on bells, in emptier air.
Scattered voices whispering.
Rows of blue-filled windows bring
sad and holy Sunday here.

In each bed a patient stares
at yellow hands on a white sheet,
hearing in his weary heart
echoes of the distant years . . .

Now the hospital's Sunday comes
in white bonnet and black gown,
saying prayers and walking round
through the white and empty rooms.

Unaware and motionless,
on his back, the old man lies,
and he fastens his flat eyes
on another emptiness.

From behind the rooftops, fast,
with the wind the swallows rise,
slice the sky, and sound their cries
like a diamond over glass.

1930-1950

Levar di sole

Cielo d'aurora su cui poso la fronte,
sei come spalla di donna, dolce.
Come viso che amico si volge,
mi arridi, sole, sorgendo dal monte.

O umana bellezza del mondo,
carne di luce promessa alla morte;
e tu, cuor di terra, che batti forte,
occulto chi sa dove, in profondo.

Sunrise

Dawn sky, on you I lean my brow
as on a woman's shoulder, sweet.
Sun, like a friend's face turned to me,
you rise from behind the mountain now.

O human beauty of the world,
flesh of the light betrothed to death,
and you, great beating heart of earth
in unimagined depths concealed.

Canzonetta d'inverno

In mezzo a un pulviscolo di perla,
tra leggiere architetture d'argento
e specchi di verde acqua ferma,
mi si è fatto un cuore di vetro.

E felice sarei, tutto chiaro
del freddo splendore che m'empie,
senz'altro senso che un vago
tremore dagli occhi alle tempie,

non fosse questo sapore
di sangue impastato alla bocca,
e il chiuso lontano dolore
d'essere stato vivo, una volta.

Winter Song

Green mirrors of water lie still,
light silvery sculptures are cast
amid a fine dusting of pearl:
I feel my heart turned into glass.

And I would be happy, suffused
with the light of this cold clarity,
with no other feeling but this
slight tremor that moves from my eye

to my temple, if not for the taste
of blood at my lips, and inside,
a buried and faraway trace
of pain, that I once was alive.

Scirocco

Mi desta a un tratto sole crudo
che riempie di fuoco bianco
il cavo del cielo, tutto nudo,
su un verde d'acque battuto e stanco.

Una vela rossa e gialla
vacilla, andando lentissimamente.
I gabbiani siedono a galla,
in frotte, su le onde sonnolente.

Dai marmi pallidi della riva
trasuda un umido tepore;
sento non so che ebrezza cattiva
entrarmi, con un riso falso, nel cuore.

C'è nell'aria mossa appena
un torbido inganno di piacere:
m'accarezzano la schiena
dita di velluto molli e leggiere.

Respiro lussuria senza amore;
son avido di gioia e infelice;
come chi tien tra le labbra un fiore,
e sente l'amaro della radice.

Scirocco

I'm suddenly awakened by
white flames of sunlight raw and hot
flooding the hollow of the sky
over green waters beaten flat.

Nearby a red and yellow sail
moves slowly, slowly undulates.
A flock of gulls is sitting still
atop the gently lapping waves.

Pale marble of the embankment sweats,
oozing a damp warmth in the sun.
A dark insidious drunkenness
insinuates itself within.

A shadow of pleasure is aloft
on the restless air: I seem to sense
along my back the feathery soft
caresses of two velvet hands.

I breathe a loveless lust, I'm sour
at heart, I hunger for the fruit
of joy, like a man who puts a flower
to his lips and tastes the bitter root.

Anacreontica

Splende la prugna dentro la frasca,
e l'aurora sopra il monte.
La ragazza ha le braccia bionde
immerse nel cielo della vasca.

L'albero bruno è una gallina
che si gonfia con tutte le penne.
La ragazza i panni distende,
scopre il petto quando si china.

Il monte è un pane sfornato or ora,
caldo, odoroso di grano e sale.
La ragazza si toglie il grembiale,
ed è tutta color dell'aurora.

C'è qualcuno che ride piano:
forse è il ruscello, forse son io.
Essa fugge, e mi dice addio
agitando la piccola mano.

Povero vecchio vagabondo,
scuoto il ramo, la prugna raccatto;
mordo, e mi sento nel sangue matto
tutta entrar la dolcezza del mondo.

Anacreontic

Dawn shines on the mountaintop, and
the glistening plum shines on the bough.
The girl plunges her ivory arms now
deep in the blue sky of the pond.

Brown trees are a flock of squat hens
with feathers all ruffled and fluffed.
The girl loosens the top of her shift
and uncovers her breast as she bends.

The mountain's a loaf, oven-warm,
still fragrant with salt and with wheat.
The girl drops her clothes at her feet,
her whole body the color of dawn.

A soft laugh comes from somewhere nearby,
perhaps from the brook, or from me.
She looks up, and runs hurriedly,
her fluttering hands waving goodbye.

I shake the branch, hold out my hand,
catch the plum, and taste the thick juice.
I feel all the world's sweetness suffuse
the mad blood of an old vagabond.

Ritratto

Ella è sola e lontana,
tra queste cose della terra,
come sul ciglio della notte estrema
la stella diana.

Non ha sapore di sangue, di sale,
di male, di donna.

Nell'ovale del viso
ogni linea par ferma
per sempre.
La bianca bocca è sigillata, senza
sorriso; agli occhi vuoti
affiora una compatta luce azzurra
d'acque profonde.
Una deserta pace
l'avvolge e chiude: intorno
nitida è l'aria come specchio;
non crolla ramo, non trema foglia,
non trema voglia o paura di carne;
anche la dolorosa
speranza tace.

Cosa inumana è questa
grande fanciulla. Pare
il termine posato da un dio
tra la memoria della vita-sogno
e l'infinito oblio.

Portrait

She is alone and apart,
amid the things of the earth,
like the morning star at the edge
of utmost night.

She has no savor of blood, of salt,
of fault, of woman.

In the oval of her face
every line seems set
forever.
Her white unsmiling mouth is sealed.
The concentrated blue
of deep waters lies on the surface of
her empty eyes.
A barren peace
surrounds her and enfolds her. Everywhere
the air is mirror-smooth.
No falling branch, no trembling leaf,
no trembling grief, fear, or desire.
Here even painful
hope has ceased.

Majestic, inanimate,
inhuman now, she seems
the boundary a god has drawn
between the memory of the life-dream
and endless oblivion.

Fiore del nulla

Quando ti schiudi, fiore
divino, assorto è il tempo
fuor di notte e di giorno;
l'aria non ha colore,
tutto è perduto intorno.
Tu solo sei, divino
fiore del nulla, amore.

Flower of Nothingness

When you are opened, blest
flower, time is absorbed
beyond all day and night,
the air is colorless
and all surroundings lost.
Then you alone exist,
love, flower of nothingness.

Autunnale

Si leva il mattino, con occhi d'oro
appannati di sonno e rugiada;
gli vanno incontro per l'aria chiara
due gabbiani con lungo volo.

In terra tutto è rimasto immoto:
la luce rade i foschi mattoni,
si posa alla pietra dei balconi,
impolvera l'acqua, risale nel vuoto.

Laggiú in fondo la riva si flette,
dolce ramo, entro un velo di brine:
le case al sole son bionde susine;
in ombra, susine violette.

Al lieve vento che vien dal mare,
piú nudi, piú tremano i pioppi,
foglie gialle, a mucchi, a groppi,
vanno con l'ombra del canale.

Il sole attraversa lento le rose
che stan sul ramo ad aspettare;
come per voglia d'accarezzare
gira attorno a tutte le cose.

La terra soffre d'un dolore
chiuso dentro, arido e muto;
pare che un bene grande, perduto
prima che amato, le stringa il cuore.

Autumnal

The day awakes, its golden eyes
still dim with slumber and with dew.
In the transparent morning, two
seagulls slowly turn and rise.

The ground below is motionless.
Light grazes the dark bricks, plays over
stone balconies and skims the water,
then rises through the emptiness.

Wrapped in a veil of mist and cold
the depths of the embankments wave.
The houses are purple plums in shade,
in sun they're plums of tawny gold.

The poplars, trembling as leaves fall,
grow naked in the light sea breeze.
The swirls and piles of yellow leaves
flee with the shadow on the canal.

The sunlight slowly falls across
the roses waiting on the vine;
it touches everything in turn,
as if in a fever to caress.

The earth endures a hidden hurt.
A barren, silent grieving for
some great and good thing, lost before
it could be loved, has seized its heart.

L'aria è piú bianca del tuo viso,
piú liscia e tepida del tuo fianco;
la rosa raccoglie un sangue stanco
piú molle e triste del tuo sorriso.

Il giorno ha schiuso le mute porte
alla sera che già sovrasta . . .
Se amore di donna piú non basta,
venga dunque amore di morte.

Ma la morte passa e non tocca.
Lascia solo un'ombra leggera
su gli occhi e su l'anima prigioniera,
e un filo d'amaro nella bocca.

The air is paler than your eyes,
smoother and warmer than your flesh.
The rose reveals a weary blush
softer and sadder than your smile.

Day opens up the silent gates,
evening already dims the sky . . .
When love of woman starts to die,
then love of death will take its place.

But death comes past and moves along
without a touch. Its shadows fall
on the eyes and the imprisoned soul,
its bitter taste lies on the tongue.

La vigna

La vigna, che ha dormito
la breve notte rorida di stelle,
si sveglia al primo battere di ciglia
del cielo di levante:
se tu premi l'orecchio su le zolle,
senti che cresce.

The Vineyard

The vineyard, that has slept
the short night dewed with stars,
awakes with the first flutter of lashes
in the eastern sky:
if you put your ear to the ground,
you can hear it growing.

I bruni olivi

I bruni olivi sottovento, e il vento
che striscia bianco al fondo della valle,
e tra la nebbia il folgorio del sole
sopra il mare invisibile. Che luogo,
che tempo è questo, o mia perduta vita?
O vita che mi segui come l'ombra,
e come l'ombra sei da me divisa.

Dark Olive Trees

Dark olive trees to leeward, and the wind
white as it skims the bottom of the valley,
and in the haze the flashing of the sun
above the invisible sea. What place is this,
what time is this I've come to? My lost life,
this life that still pursues me like a shadow,
and like a shadow stands apart from me.

Primavera

Sotto la fuga leggera del vento
s'apre il ventaglio del mandorlo bianco.
Alto sta un cielo di rosa e d'argento.
Ma il cuore è stanco.

Spring

The white fan of the chestnut tree is spread
under the wind's fugue, delicate and merry.
A pink and silver sky is overhead.
But the heart is weary.

Su la riva del sonno

Su la riva del sonno alterne voci
odo alzarsi dal mare:
il tonfo sordo dell'onda che viene,
l'acuto scroscio dell'onda che va.
E il cuore è come un sasso,
trascinato dal suo cieco destino
a rotolare e a stridere tra i sassi
su la riva del sonno.

On the Shore of Sleep

On the shore of sleep I hear successive
voices rising from the sea:
the dull plash of the wave that comes,
the sharp crack of the wave that goes.
And the heart is like a stone,
dragged by its blind destiny
to roll and crash among the stones
on the shore of sleep.

Mare

Mare, sotto il tuo silenzio forte
appena incrinato dalle piccole onde
ascolto il segreto succhiar delle fonde
correnti, rapinose come la morte.

Cosí m'inviti tu, sempre amato,
tu, amaro, che ancora mi ami:
cosí, dolente eterno, a te chiami
il mio cuor gonfio d'annegato.

Sea

Sea, underneath your massive silence
the small waves barely ruffle, in the depth
I hear the secret sucking of the currents,
savage and passionate as death.

You I have always loved, who love me too,
I hear you beckoning, o bitter sea:
I hear you, sorrowing eternally,
summon my drowned and swollen heart to you.

Campo di esilio

Percossi sradicati alberi siamo,
ritti ma spenti, e questa avara terra
che ci porta non è la nostra terra.
Intorno a noi la roccia soffa vènti
nemici, fuma opache ombre di nubi,
aspri soli lampeggia da orizzonti
di verdi ghiacci. Le nostre segrete
radici, al caldo al gelo, nude tremano.
E intanto il tempo volge per il cielo
i mattini le sere: alte deserte
stagioni: e i lumi del ricordo, e i fuochi
della speranza, e i pazzi arcobaleni.
Come morti aspettiamo che la morte
passi; e l'un l'altro ci guardiamo, strani,
con occhi d'avvizzite foglie. E un tratto
trasaliamo stupiti, se alla cima
di un secco ramo un germoglio si schiuda,
e la corteccia senta urgere al labbro
delle vecchie ferite un sangue vivo;
tra le nubi scorrendo un dolce vento
di primavere nostre.

Di qua c'è un mattino color d'aurora
fermo àlle rive di ghiaccio del mondo.
Di là c'è un piccolo viso biondo
che trema come una tenera rosa.

Un pallido viso scavato alle guance
di là dai ghiacci incendiati d'oro.
Di là dagli spazi senza suono
la musica di un cuore che piange.

Exile Camp

We are all battered and uprooted trees,
upright but dead, and this unyielding land,
bare soil that bears our weight, is not our land.
And all about us now the rock exhales
the enemy winds, and puffs up solid shadows
of clouds, and sets ablaze the bitter suns
above the horizons of green ice. Our secret
roots shiver naked to the heat and cold.
Above us the high hand of time rotates
mornings and evenings through the sky,
those empty, distant seasons. And the lights
of memory, and the fires of hope, and all
the crazy rainbows. Like the dead we wait
for death to pass. And, strangers, we all stare
at one another with eyes like shriveled leaves.
Suddenly we all start with astonishment
as a bud bursts into blossom at the tip
of a dry branch, and the bark feels living blood
come surging to the lip of its old wounds—
a soft wind of our seedtimes blowing now
between the clouds.

On this side morning colored with the dawn
sits motionless above the shores of ice.
On the other side a tiny face
that trembles like a rose upon the vine.

A pale light-colored face with hollow cheeks
beyond the ice inflamed with golden rays.
Beyond the cold and silent space
the tender music of a heart that weeps.

Il giorno è nero di corvi e ricordi,
di tonfi sordi, di passi di morti.
La notte ha il viso dell'amore vicino.
La notte è un volo di bianche colombe.

Tu, corpo senza peso, paurosa dolcezza
di braccia come ali, di mani come fiori,
tremar di palpebre basse, tenere labbra incolori,
capelli come un'erba bionda di sole e d'altezza.

Tu da cosí lontana lontananza venuta,
coi tuoi piccoli passi di smarrita fanciulla,
dentro la notte immensa e chiusa come il nulla,
a posar sul mio petto quest'angoscia tua muta.

Poi lenta levi il capo, e mi fissi negli occhi
gli occhi tuoi nudi, fondi, innamorati dentro,
e allora mi travolge la rapina d'un vento
di luce, e mi consuma come nuvola a fiocchi.

Poi non ci fu che neve, sepolta
dissolta ogni forma: quel bianco morto,
quel molle soffocato ricordo
d'un mondo morto con la sua colpa.

Non c'era piú cuore, sangue: soltanto
un delirare dell'anima chiusa
dentro la morte, con la delusa
sua luce, col cane del suo peccato.

The day is black with crows and memories,
with dull thuds, footsteps of the dead.
The night draws near and wears the face of love.
The night is the huge wing of a white dove.

You, body without weight, you, sweet and timid one
with hands like little flowers, arms like tender wings,
lips soft and colorless, and eyelids fluttering,
and hair like grasses bleached by altitude and sun.

You, with your tiny footsteps of a child who's lost,
sealed up like nothingness in night's immensity,
from an impossible distance coming here to me
to lay your silent anguish down upon my breast.

You slowly lift your head, and then I am transfixed
by your deep and unveiled eyes that hold their love within,
and suddenly I'm stripped and shaken by a wind
of light, consumed as if by a white cloud thick with flakes.

Then nothing but snowfall: it blurred
and buried each shape as it left
dead white memories, smothered and soft,
of a world that was guilty and dead.

No blood anymore, the heart gone:
now nothing at all but soul raving,
soul sealed in its death, with its fading
light, with the hound of its sin.

Seme di cenere sotto la neve.
E i giorni morti passavano invano.
La bellezza moriva lontano,
a impossibili rive serene.

Seeds of ashes under the snows.
Day following meaningless day.
Beauty had died far away,
on serene and impossible shores.

1950-1965: I

Risveglio

L'odore mattutino
degli alberi, e le strisce
verdi nel cielo bianco cenerino . . .
I miei sensi si allungan come bisce
a toccare le cose, a discoprire
dietro le cose le antiche memorie,
le incredibili storie
dell'ieri, del domani, del morire.

Waking

The scent of trees
in the morning, and the streaks
of green across the white and ashy skies . . .
My senses stretch themselves like little snakes
trying to touch things, trying to unearth
beneath the things the ancient memories,
the incredible histories
of yesterdays, of days to come, of death.

Passaggio

Lungo la spiaggia di sabbia fina,
su l'orlo di un mare a pecorelle,
lento procede in triplice fila
un branchettino di paperelle.

Vanno di passo regolare
come un collegio di chierichini,
girano solo la testa a beccare
i pallidi insetti salterini.

Dietro c'è un mare che freme selvaggio,
sopra c'è un sole che avvampa in leone.
Restano, a segno del lieve passaggio,
tante crocette a fior del sabbione.

In Passing

Across the stretch of sandy coast,
along the edge of a fleecy ocean,
a flock of goslings, three abreast,
marches in slow and steady motion.

They move in step, deliberately,
like a college of ecclesiasts,
and snap at the somersaultery
of pallid insects skipping past.

Below a sun that burns the sky,
beside wild waves that wash the land,
they leave the sign of their passing by,
a host of crosses on the sand.

Fil di vento

Le buie strade, e il sole nelle piazze,
e il mondo . . . E gl'infiniti
spazi e silenzi.
E gli umani fantasmi. E il tempo, come
un fil di vento a fiore delle cose.

Blade of Wind

The dark roads, and the sunlight in the courtyards,
and the world . . . And the infinite
spaces and silences.
And the human ghosts. And time, like a smooth blade
of wind along the edge of everything.

Fredda ancora l'aria

Fredda ancora l'aria, i cieli duri.
Ma già la terra fuma, soffocata
da desideri oscuri:
sotto il velo dell'erba appena nata,
brucia e suda, e rabbrividisce nuda.

The Air Still Chilly

The air still chilly, and still harsh the skies.
But the earth is already smoldering with suppressed
and dark desires:
under the veil of newborn grass it burns
and sweats, and shivers in its nakedness.

1950-1965: II

Estate in cielo

Il grande carre coruscante d'oro
va traballando per l'alto, con lampi
vorticosi di ruote. Col suo vento
di fiamma leva polvere di nuvole,
arriccia l'aride chiome del monte;
al piano imbianca le cime dei pioppi,
brucia i fiumi assetati che si celano
tra lividi pietroni, fa impazzire
le diafane cicale abbarbicate
ad ogni ombra di rama. (Ma non tocca
il rondinino nero, affusolato,
posato all'orlo della sua grondaia.)

Passa il carro col giorno; se lo ingoia
la notte. Ora esso è fermo, impiccolito,
lassú lontano, punteggiato d'oro
nella tenebra, col timone alzato,
tra un crepitio di spighe intorno sparse.

Summer Sky

The Great Wain with its sparkling points of gold
goes swaying through the heavens, sending swirls
of lightning flashes from its turning wheels.
With its wind of flame it lifts the dust of clouds,
sifts the dry hair along the mountainsides.
It bleaches the tips of poplars in the fields,
scorches the thirsty streams that hide themselves
amid the huge and livid rocks, and drives
the diaphanous cicadas, clinging to
the shadow of every branch, to madness. (Yet
it doesn't touch the tiny swallow, black
and tapered, poised on the edge of the gutter pipe.)

The wain goes with the day. The night has come
to swallow it. Now it is still, grown small,
high in the distant sky, its points of gold
shining in darkness, with its shaft upraised,
amid the crackling of the scattered stalks.

Solitudine

Solitudine dura e cara,
compagna dei miei tardi giorni,
alla mensa d'erba amara,
al torbo vino dei ricordi,

soli siamo, tu ed io.
Pur non è triste il nostro stato:
una dolcezza lenta di oblío
già impolvera e copre il passato.

E fuori ride un cielo puro,
splende il prato di tenere erbe.
Ancora sui rami del futuro
la speranza ha fior del verde.

Solitude

Solitude hard and dear,
mate of these late days of mine,
with the bitter herbs spread here,
with memories' muddy wine,

we are alone, you and I.
Our life is not sad, nonetheless:
the past has been dust-coated by
a sweet slow forgetfulness.

A clear sky laughs over the house,
soft green gives the field a sheen.
And still on the future's boughs
hope shows a flower of green.

Acquarello

Come leggera e tenera si posa
su te la luce. Si posa e si avvolge
al puro braccio, segnandolo netto
dentro contorni candidi, la spalla
inombrando di rosa.
Nel cavo dell'ascella, ombra di seta,
affiora la tua molle ombra segreta.

Watercolor

How tenderly, caressingly the light
settles upon you. Settles and entwines
about your smooth arm, neatly filling in
its clean outlines, and shadowing your shoulder
with a flush of pink.
In the hollow of your armpit, shadowed in silk,
your own soft secret shadow comes to light.

Estate di Roma

Su la terra nerastra,
trito ossame di secoli,
trema e sfavilla l'erba di un mattino.
Sotto gli archi degli acquedotti rossi
si scolorano i teneri oleandri.
Nel cielo alto s'impennano
nuvole tese dal caldo vento,
come sul colle d'oro i candidi
cavalli dei Dioscuri.

Roman Summer

On the blackish earth,
ground bones of centuries,
grass shivers and sparkles in the morning.
Under the arches of red aqueducts
the tender oleander fades.
Clouds stretched by the warm wind
rear in the high sky
like the white horses of the Dioscuri
over the golden hills.

Ricordo di Gallipoli

Cosí forte il meriggio sopra il mare,
che i muri della stanza
si schiudevano come valve d'oro.
Fiammavano sul lino
candido il vino e l'olio. E tu movevi
lente dita di luce nella luce
a ravviarti i lucenti capelli.

Remembrance of Gallipoli

The blaze of noon so strong upon the sea
the walls of the room
were opened up like walls of golden valve.
On the white linen
the oil and wine were flaming. In the light
slowly you moved your long fingers of light
to rearrange your hair alive with light.

From *Verità di uno* (1970)

Mitologia

Questa pioggia d'estate,
muta minuta calda,
penetra fronda e zolla,
fa della terra carne.

Come una Danae bagnata d'amore,
soffusa gli occhi d'ombra,
s'apre la valle supina.
Giove è già in alto, lontano,
invisibile dietro la nube.

Mythology

This summer rain,
silent slow and warm,
penetrates bush and turf,
turns earth to flesh.

Like a Danae wet with love,
eyes suffused with shadow,
supine, the valley lies open.
Jove is already far, on high,
invisible behind the clouds.

A Domenico Cantatore

Ho visto i tuoi paesi, la tua terra
scura, colline in ombra, campi grigi
irti di sassi, boscaglie di ulivi,
la tua terra colore dell'oliva,
come l'oliva amara. In alto, cieli
di fuoco bianco e tutt'intorno un mare
di zaffiro e di giada. Ho visto donne
chiuse entro nere bende o nere chiome,
pallida carne calda, ombrosi sguardi
con scintille profonde. Ho in me l'amore
tuo, la tristezza tua, della tua terra,
quella gran luce vuota, quei silenzi
di attesa, dei tuoi cieli.

To Domenico Cantatore

I have seen your villages, your countrysides,
your dark earth, hills in shadow, your gray fields
bristling with stones, your groves of olive trees,
your earth the color of an olive, of
a bitter olive. High above, the skies
streaked with white flame, and everywhere a sea
of jade and sapphire. I have seen the women
wrapped in their black kerchiefs or their black hair,
warm alabaster flesh, and shadowed looks
with deep and searching sparks. Within myself
I have your love, your sadness, for your earth,
that wide and empty light, those silences
of waiting, of your skies.

Forse, un giorno, così...

Il canale si gonfia e si dilata;
soverchia a uno a uno
i gradini d'approdo, si distende,
lucido, eguale,
su la riva di pietra, e cresce e cresce.

Forse, un giorno, sarà così la fine
di questa favola d'acqua e di sasso.
Inghiottita dal fango e dalle sabbie
molli, trasparirà sotto una lastra
di cristallo verdino: lei che fu
lo splendore del mondo,
incantato miraggio
su l'inquieto deserto del mare;
dolce morta, ora,
supina nella luce
con tutti gli ori e i fuochi delle gemme
che un tempo la vestirono,
basilissa raggiante, troppo bella
per durare nel tempo,
fatta per esser morta.

Venezia, 6 novembre 1966

One Day, Perhaps, This Way . . .

The canal fills and swells,
overwhelming one by one
the steps of the landing, spreading,
sparkling and even, over
the stone shore, rising and rising.

One day, perhaps, it will end this way,
this legend made of water and of rock.
Swallowed up by mud and soft
sands, she will lie beneath a transparent sheet
of greenish crystal: she who was
the glory of the world,
an enchanting mirage
in the restless desert of the sea,
now sweetly dead,
supine in the light
of all the gold and the flaming gems
time dressed her in,
a gleaming basilissa, too beautiful
to last through time,
created to be dead.

Venice, 6 November 1966

Il fico

Laggiù al paese, nell'orto,
i miei mattini erano sul fico
largo di foglie, bruno, chiazzato
di neri frutti. Mi nascondevo nel folto
del grande albero amico. Il sole
montava alto, più alto del fico,
di me sul fico.
Guardavo il mondo, l'orto del vicino,
di là dal muro. Ogni tanto coglievo
un frutto, che gemeva latte
dal picciuolo spezzato e sangue denso
dalla ferita di sotto.
Ero un piccolo Pan, gracile, anemico,
nel primo sboccio timido dei sensi;
re del mondo, dell'orto;
il solo vivo su la terra
nel tutto mio mattino d'estate.

The Fig Tree

Down in the country, in the orchard,
I'd spend my mornings in the fig tree
broadleafed and brown and spotted
with black fruit. I would hide in the thickness of
the great friendly tree. The sun
would climb high in the sky, higher than the tree
and me in the tree.
With the orchard all around, I'd gaze at the world
beyond the wall. Every now and then I'd pick
a fig that trickled milk
from the small break where I'd plucked it, and thick blood
from the wound I gave it.
I was a tiny Pan, anemic, frail,
in the first bashful blossoming of the senses,
the king of the world, of the orchard,
in all my wide summer morning
the only living thing on earth.

From *Calle del vento* (1975)

Qui c'è sempre un poco di vento,
a tutte l'ore, di ogni stagione:
un soffio almeno, un respiro.
Qui da tanti anni sto io, ci vivo.
E giorno dopo giorno scrivo
il mio nome sul vento.

Here there's always a bit of wind,
all hours, every season,
a puff at least, a breath.
Here I've lived so long, here I stay.
And I write day after day
my name on the wind.

Sotto l'albero, qui,
tra un tremare di verdi ombre, come acque,
e flagranti occhi di sole,
passa il mattino d'estate, passa
l'estate con la sua felicità.
Felicità di vaste arie, di nubi
grondanti luce,
di frutti d'oro appesi a rami d'oro.
Felicità del vecchio cuore,
vivo, in amore.

Under the tree, here,
between green shadows rippling like a stream
and the flagrant eyes of the sun,
the summer morning passes, the summer
passes with its happiness.
Happiness of the wide air, of the clouds
dripping light,
of the gold fruit hanging on the golden boughs.
Happiness of the old heart,
alive, in love.

Per tutto il cielo dilaga la sera.
L'ombra ch'è ancora luce
penetra nella luce
ch'è già polvere d'ombra.
È la sera: il colore
smarrito della sera,
il volto umano della sera,
la mortale dolcezza della sera.

Evening spreads across the sky.
Shadow that's still light
penetrates the light
that's already dust of shadow.
It's evening: the lost
color of evening,
the human face of evening,
the fatal sweetness of evening.

Al mio tempo fanciullo
primavera non era
il sole nuovo, il vento nuovo
la nuova rosa color di rosa
in vetta al verde spino.
Era il lombrico biondo o bruno
che si torceva furibondo
tra la zolla nerastra, umida, liscia . . .
Io scavavo con la mia zappetta
nel piccolo orto. Appariva quel mostro
incantevole e orrendo:
era il mistero della vita, la segreta
meraviglia della primavera.

Back when I was a boy
spring never meant for me
the new sun, the new breeze,
the new rose-colored rose
on the top of the green thornbush.
Spring was the earthworm, brown or pale,
twisting furiously through
the damp, the smooth dark soil . . .
I would go digging with my tiny hoe
in the little kitchen garden—and there he was,
the horrible wonderful beast:
he was the mystery of life, the secret
miracle of the spring.

Saba, Stuparich, Giotti
e l'Anita Pittoni (e la sua gatta).
E la bora furiosa per le strade,
e il mare in piazza.
E le splendide *mule*, a schiera, in danza,
su e giù per il Corso . . .

Trieste è stata una calda stagione
della mia vita. Sul fumoso orizzonte
della memoria
ancora manda lampi.

Saba, Stuparich, Giotti,
and Anita Pittoni (and her cat).
And the northwind slashing through the avenues,
and the sea in the marketplace.
And the row of marvelous mules, and how they danced
all up and down the Corso . . .

Trieste is forever a warm season
of my life. On the smoky horizon
of memory
I still can see it flashing.

Primavera tenera e acerba
di rude bigello vestita,
spruzzata di pioggia, di sole . . .
Come quella ragazza
che incontrai su per le scale
del condominio vecchio.
Scendeva a colpo di vento,
nuda il collo sul nascere del petto.
Sotto il suo aspro camicione grigio
certo era nuda tutta, e scintillante.

Springtime tender and unripe
dressed in her coarse homespun,
splashed with rain, with sun . . .
Like the girl
who passed me on the steps
of the old apartment house.
She came down in a gust of wind,
bared to the budding of her breasts.
Under her rough gray blouse, I knew,
she was glowing in her nakedness.

Te ne sei andata, lasciandoti dietro
un lungo sguardo come smarrito:
un po' della tua anima, mi è parso.
Forse era un moto di gentile pietà,
o forse una piccola ansia d'amore.
Certo era un dono di te, che lasciavi
a chi restava, solo,
nel vuoto dove prima eri tu.

Now you have gone away, leaving behind
a long look, like something lost:
a little bit of your soul, it seemed to me.
Perhaps it was a tender pulse of pity,
perhaps a sudden fluttering of love.
Surely it was a gift you left
for the one who stayed,
alone, with the emptiness that once was you

Giro del sole nelle nostre stanze,
da finestra a finestra, da mattino
a sera. Quanti giorni, quante
stagioni, e poi anni . . .
Le nostre figlie bambine, poi donne.
Tu sempre più stanca e lontana,
poi finita, una mattina all'alba.
Io qui ancora, a guardare stupito
il tempo che gira
col vecchio sole da finestra a finestra.

The movement of the sun across our rooms
from window to window, from the morning
to the evening. How many days, how many
seasons, and then years . . .
Our little girls, then women.
You ever more weary and far, and then
all over, one morning at dawn.
I still here, to watch in astonishment
time as it moves
through window after window with the old sun.

Il bel sole si stende eguale
su la pianura che al lago dichina.
Il bel sole sente ora la stanchezza
del lungo corso, al settembre si piega.
C'è nell'aria una immota attesa. E rondini
non se ne vede già più.
Che dice l'albero grande
gonfio ancora di tutte le sue foglie?
Non dice nulla. Attende.

Come noi. Come noi che un tempo fummo
giovani qui, su questo lago,
pazzo di luce alta, noi pazzi
di speranza. Ora la luce cala,
e le speranze sono sparite,
come le rondini impazienti
della tarda estate.

Fine sunlight spreads evenly
on the plain that slopes down to the lake.
Bending into September, the sun
feels the weariness of the long road.
The air is still with waiting. And already
there are no swallows to be seen.
What does the tall tree say,
still swollen with all its leaves?
Nothing at all. It waits.

Like us. Like us who once upon a time
were young here, on this lake
crazed with light, as we were crazed
with hope. Now the light falls,
the hopes have fled away
like the swallows impatient with
the sluggish summer.

Io vidi già sotto un cielo d'inferno
rotto avvampato dai fuochi di guerra
schiudersi la corolla di una rosa
bianca, amorosa.
Tra i rombi che squarciavano la notte
udivo il suono lene di un ruscello
mosso tra l'erba e i sassi. Nell'orrore
di morte solo era vivo quel suono
d'acqua, e quel fiore.

Once long ago under a hellish sky
ripped and shrieking with the flames of war
I saw the corolla of a pure white rose
gently unclose.
In all the roars that tore the night apart
faintly I heard the flowing of a stream
rustling past grass and rocks. And in the horror
of death, the only live things were that sound
of water and that flower.

Quella vecchia vecchia storia,
questo pianto senza fine.
Storia di un uomo e di una donna,
vecchia come il mondo.
Ma al tempo che fu nostro,
essa fu solo nostra,
e segreta e splendente:
storia vera come la morte.
E fu infatti la morte a dire
la parola suprema,
la verità,
di quel nostro sognare la vita.

That old old story,
these endless tears.
A story of a man and a woman,
old as the world.
But while it was ours
it was ours alone,
secret and shimmering,
a story true as death.
And it was death to speak
the final word,
the truth,
on the dream that was our life.

Si cammina sul filo degli anni
da esperti funamboli.
È un difficile andare, ma si va.
E intanto il mondo, attorno,
muta faccia e colore. Senza posa
ogni creata cosa
in poco d'ora ci diventa strana.
E con le cose ci mutiamo noi,
d'oggi in domani.
Solo sta fermo nel fondo di noi
quel nostro tempo primo,
l'infanzia, all'ombra della madre, sotto
il crocifisso piccolo di avorio.

We make our way along the thread of years
like expert tightrope walkers.
The going's difficult, but on we go.
Meanwhile the world about us
keeps changing face and color. Ceaselessly
each created thing we see
in a drop of time grows strange before our eyes.
And with the things we're changing in ourselves,
today into tomorrow.
All that stays fixed, down deep inside ourselves,
is that first time we knew,
when we were little children, in mother's shadow,
under the little ivory crucifix.

I giorni, i mesi, gli anni,
dove mai sono andati?
Questo piccolo vento
che trema alla mia porta,
uno a uno, in silenzio,
se li è portati via.
Questo piccolo vento
foglia a foglia mi spoglia
dell'ultimo mio verde
già spento. E così sia.

The days, the months, the years,
where have they disappeared?
This little bit of wind
that trembles at my door,
in silence, one by one,
has taken them from me.
This little bit of wind
has stripped me leaf by leaf
of my last bit of green.
It's gone. And let it be.

From *Poesie inedite, o "come"* (1977)

A Venezia, posata sul suo letto
d'acque marine e d'ali di gabbiani,
la primavera scende da una nuvola
grande, carica d'ombra, orlata d'oro.
E' la fine improvvisa di febbraio;
è l'ora che Venezia si ridesta
alla luce, al colore. Sul suo volto
amoroso trascorrono pallori,
veli violetti, lampi di rossore;
ai suoi piedi si stendon le maree
come giardini: a Venezia, di marzo,
anche l'acqua dà fiore.

In Venice, as it rests upon its bed
of waters from the sea and seagulls' wings,
the spring descends from out of a great cloud,
charged with shadow, hemmed with threads of gold.
Suddenly it's the end of February,
the time when Venice wakes, and stirs itself
once more to light and color. Now across
the city's affectionate face pass all the pallors,
the violet veils, the blush of lightning flashes,
and at the city's feet tides spread themselves
like gardens. In Venice, in the month of March,
even the water's in bloom.

E così mi son fermato
ai piedi del ponte.
E così ti sei fermata anche tu
un gradino più su.
Non sapevo ch'era un addio.
L'ho saputo un attimo dopo
sentendo le tue labbra sfiorare le mie.
Era la prima, era l'ultima volta.
Così.

And so I stopped
at the foot of the bridge.
And so you stopped as well
on the step above.
I didn't know it was farewell.
I knew it a moment later
when I felt your lips brush lightly against mine.
It was the first, it was the last time.
So.

Tu che hai occhi per vedere i miracoli,
guarda la gemma apparsa sul ramo
dell'alberello nudo stecchito.
E' un punto, è un nulla.
Ma è già il suo fiore, il suo frutto,
la sua morte, la sua resurrezione.

You who have eyes to witness miracles,
look at the bud emerging on the bare
branch of the brittle sapling.
It's a dot, a bit of nothing,
and yet already its flower and its fruit,
already its death and its resurrection.

Con lo sguardo immutato
dell'ultima tua sera
tu mi segui, ombra viva,
da dietro l'ombre morte,
mentre io vo misurando
questi miei anni lunghi.
Tu che avesti anni brevi,
tu che fosti il soave
fiore d'una stagione,
segui me, vecchio errante
tra memorie di sogni
e sogni di memorie:
tu, mia morta dolcezza,
tu, mio dolore amato.
Sguardo vivo, dolente
senza lacrime, dolce
senza sorriso, seguimi,
seguimi fin che duri
un barlume di giorno
su questa buia strada
che alla svolta s'affretta.
Alla svolta . . . alla svolta .

With the look upon your face
unchanged from your last evening
you follow me, living shadow,
behind all the dead shadows,
while I go measuring
all these long years of mine.
You whose years were short,
you who were the soft
bloom of a season, follow
this old man wandering
between memories of dreams
and dreams of memories:
you, my departed sweetness,
you, my beloved sorrow.
A living look, sorrowful
without a tear, and sweet
without a smile, you follow,
follow me till the last
glimmering of the daylight
along this darkening street
that hastens to a turning.
To a turning . . . to a turning . . .

From *Tempo e Poesia* (1964)

Il vecchio poeta e il suo libro

Impresa non facile né allegra quella di uno scrittore, diciamo pure un poeta, diciamo meglio un vecchio poeta, che, per generoso invito dell'amico editore, si trovi a dover raccogliere in un solo volume, probabilmente ultimo, certamente già definitivo, le poesie da lui scritte nel corso di un mezzo secolo di attività. Codeste poesie, consegnate via via, come le foglie di Virgilio, ai vènti passeggeri della cronaca, fanno ora un bel mucchio di carte, da affidare (o Dio!) ai monsoni della storia (letteraria).

Rileggendo se stesso sulle bozze di stampa (poco meno di quattrocento pagine), il vecchio poeta è travagliato da due sentimenti distinti, se non contradittorî: tristezza, perché tutto il suo mondo appartiene ormai al passato e perché di tanta fiamma non resta piú che un focherello di brage; tenerezza per quel suo povero passato, e per il focherello di parole che non vuole spegnersi, che vorrebbe anzi perpetuarsi, perpetuando in sé il tempo che fu.

Un foglietto dopo l'altro, il libro evoca giorni sereni e giorni oscuri, dalla prima giovinezza all'altrieri: paesaggi della realtà e del sogno, creature amate e perdute, tutta una vita «de fleurs, de femmes et de douleurs parée». (Appunto gli è tornata a mente la frase di un poeta caro alla sua adolescenza.) È un patetico viaggio di mille e uno ritorni; o piuttosto un assorto errare tra ombre, in un labirinto illuminato dal bianco sole della memoria.

Ma poi, ecco che l'autore-lettore si fa, com'è necessario e inevitabile, a considerare i suoi fogli con occhio critico; cercando di vederli da straniero, come se non fossero suoi; sforzandosi di giudicarli dal punto di vista estetico. E allora egli viene a trovarsi, su per giú, nello stato d'animo . . . dell'Innominato alla vigilia della conversione.

«Le sue scelleratezze», racconta il Manzoni, gli si

The Old Poet and His Book

Neither easy nor pleasant is the task facing a writer, let us say a poet, more precisely an old poet, who, through the generous offer of a publisher friend, finds himself with the job of collecting into a single volume, probably his last, certainly definitive, the poems he has written in the course of half a century of activity. Those poems, consigned along the way, like the leaves in Virgil, to the fleeting winds of newsprint, now make a fine heap of pages, to be entrusted (good God!) to the monsoons of (literary) history.

Rereading himself in galleys (a bit less than four hundred pages), the old poet is struck by two distinct, if not contradictory, feelings: sadness, because by now his whole world belongs to the past and because nothing remains of all his fire except a glow of embers; fondness for that past, and for that glow that wishes not to be extinguished, that wishes instead to perpetuate itself, perpetuating in itself the time that was.
Sheet after small sheet, the book evokes clear days and dark, from earliest youth to the day before yesterday: landscapes of reality and of dream, creatures loved and lost, an entire life *"de fleurs, de femmes, et de douleurs parée."* (The phrase of a poet dear to him in his youth comes back into his mind.) It is a sentimental journey with a thousand and one detours; or, rather, it is an absorbed wandering among shadows, in a labyrinth illuminated by the white sun of memory.
But then, as is necessary and inevitable, the author-reader brings himself to look at his pages with a critical eye; trying to see them as if they were not his own; striving to judge them from an aesthetic point of view. And then he comes to find himself in approximately the state of mind . . . of the Unnamed on the eve of his conversion.
"His crimes," says Manzoni, seemed to his mind "ugly

presentavano all'animo «brutte e troppe»: «era come il crescere e crescere d'un peso già incomodo . . .».

Su per giú, beninteso. Poiché lo scrivere poesie non è mai stato una scelleratezza, neppure agli occhi del moralista piú bigotto, neppure al cospetto della piú ombroso e rigorosa autocoscienza. E, d'altra parte, non ci sarà mai un poeta che si senta di condannare irremissibilmente, valga o non valga, l'opera sua.

Ciò nondimeno, è pur vero che il vecchio poeta, giunto al difficile passo della ricapitolazione, se non del pentimento e della conversione, non può non chiedersi: «Che cosa ho mai fatto? Questo sarebbe il frutto di una vita? Questo, insomma, sarei io, davanti alla Poesia?»

È incredibile come a una lettura cosí condizionata tutto appaia diverso e disforme rispetto alla realtà vissuta, non solo, ma anche rispetto al giudizio che il poeta avrà pur pronunciato dentro di sé nel momento della scrittura e della prima pubblicazione.

Egli, ora, davanti al gran cumulo di carte (da rimandare "con cortese sollecitudine" all'editore) si sente talmente confuso e scoraggiato, che avrebbe voglia di non farne piú nulla. Senonché, a buon punto, lo soccorre il ricordo dei critici amici e dei poeti confratelli che, attraverso tanti anni, gli hanno testimoniato la loro stima e simpatia; ed erano, e sono, fior di galantuomini: amici e confratelli bensí, ma incapaci di dire la bugia, foss'anche la "pietosa bugia."

—Possibile che si siano sbagliati tutti? Se essi han trovato del buono nelle mie cose, non dovrei trovarcelo io?

and too many": "what was already a troublesome burden was growing heavier and heavier . . ."

Approximately, of course. For the writing of poetry has never been a crime, not even in the eyes of the most bigoted moralist, not even in the view of the most sensitive and severe self-consciousness. And, on the other hand, there will never be a poet who desires to condemn his own works without reprieve, whether they deserve it or not.

Nonetheless, it is still true that the old poet, having come to the difficult step of recapitulation, if not of repentance and conversion, cannot help asking himself: "What have I ever accomplished? Is this the fruit of an entire lifetime? Is this finally what I am, in the eyes of Poetry?"

It is incredible how a reading so conditioned links together everything that was varied and diverse, not only with respect to a lived reality, but also with respect to the author's private judgment at the time of writing and of first publication.

Now, with the great heap of pages before him (to be returned to the publisher "at your earliest convenience"), he feels so confused and disheartened that he could wish never to write again—if not for a timely recollection of the friendly critics and fellow poets who have shown their affection and esteem through so many years; and they were, and are, thoroughly honest men: friends and colleagues, certainly, but incapable of a lie, even a little white one.

—Is it possible that they are all mistaken? If they have found merit in my things, shouldn't I find it there as well?

Non dovrei star quieto al loro giudizio? Va' a vedere che, sotto la tonaca dell'*umiliato*, son pieno a scoppiare di orgoglio luciferino . . .

Il poeta riprende con una talquale fiducia la sua lettura. Ma un altro pensiero súbito lo assale, risospingendolo al dubbio, alla paura. All'Innominato tutti quei delitti "brutti e troppi" ricomparivano, nell'ora critica, "separati dai sentimenti che li avevan fatti volere e commettere"; cosí al poeta, ora, le sue vecchie poesie: disambientate, immotivate, nude e crude. Non brutte, a dire vero; ma troppe, certamente, sí.

—Eppure ne ho sacrificate quasi altrettante di quelle salvate. Forse che non basta? Avrei dovuto essere anche piú duro, anche piú spietato? Comunque sia, devo ammettere, e francamente ammetto, che, specie in gioventú, ho peccato anch'io d'incontinenza verbale, di facilità canora. (Era il tempo del D'Annunzio, del Pascoli . . .) Piú tardi ho tentato di tirarmi fuori dal peccato, e credo di esserci, fino a un certo punto, riuscito . . . Basta: *quod factum infectum fieri non potest*. Il libro è quel che è; né io voglio o posso rinnegarlo. Non voglio soprattutto per questo: che, qualunque esso sia, è pur sempre un libro di buona fede. L'esame di coscienza, a cui la composizione di esso mi ha obbligato, mi lascia tranquillo a questo riguardo. Nel mio libro non c'è posa, non c'è astuzia, non c'è conformismo, non c'è anticonformismo, non c'è estusiasmo ideologico per partito preso, non c'è sperimentalismo modaiolo, non c'è nessuna menzogna, né morale né artistica. Di ciò sono abbastanza sicuro. E spero perciò che il candido lettore vorrà perdonarmi i difetti, siano artistici siano morali, che porto stampati in fronte e che non avrei potuto dissimulare se non col mentire prima a me stesso e poi a lui. Un'altra cosa

Shouldn't I submit quietly to their judgment? I begin to see that, under the cassock of humility, I am full to bursting with Luciferian pride.

Thus the poet confidently resumes his reading. But all at once another thought assails him, driving him back to doubt, to fear. In his hour of crisis, all those "ugly and too many" misdeeds reappeared to the Unnamed, "separate from the feelings that had made him desire and commit them"; in just this way his old poems now appear to the poet: fragmentary, unmotivated, bare and crude. Not ugly, to tell the truth; but too many, yes, absolutely.
—And yet I have sacrificed almost as many as I have saved. Perhaps it's not enough? Should I have been even more rigorous, more ruthless? However that may be, I should admit, and I do freely admit, that I have also sinned, especially when young, through verbal incontinence, through melodious facility. (It was the age of D'Annunzio, of Pascoli . . .) Later I tried to free myself of that sin, and I believe that, up to a certain point, I succeeded . . . Enough: *quod factum infectum fieri non potest*. The book is what it is; I neither could nor would want to disown it, for one reason above all: that, whatever else it may be, it is always a book of good faith. An examination of conscience, to which its composition has compelled me, leaves me at peace in this regard. In my book there is no pose, there is no trickery, there is no conformity, there is no anticonformity, there is no ideological enthusiasm for any party or point of view, there is no modish experimentalism, there is no lying of any kind, either moral or artistic. Of this much I am convinced. And I therefore hope that the honest reader will forgive me for the defects, whether artistic or moral, that I bear stamped upon my brow and that I could not hide without lying first to myself and then to him. I

spero e mi auguro: che attraverso tutto il volume egli possa scoprire il corso di un'unica vena di sentimento e di pensiero: e una specie di coerenza o costanza tonale; e una ostinata aspirazione a una forma di semplici linee e di significati trasparenti: insomma l'impronta di *uno*. Di uno che non ha il furore del nuovo, che anzi gode di sentirsi dentro la tradizione poetica del proprio paese, della propria terra; di uno che crede, anche in questi caotici tempi, alla sacertà della bellezza, come ci credette il Petrarca padre (in tempi, del resto, non meno caotici dei nostri). Cosí sia, cosí sia. Solamente, vorrei pregarlo, il candido lettore, di cominciare la lettura del mio libro dalla terza o dalla seconda parte. Cosí troverebbe, poi, meno ingiustificabili i miei antichi peccati: *peccata iuventutis meae*.

Con tali o altrettali parole, silenziosamente dette a se stesso, il vecchio poeta, seduto davanti alla montagnola delle sue bozze di stampa, si conforta come può e quanto basta per portare a termine la sua lettura, la sua fatica.

Ecco: le bozze son tutte corrette. Domattina le spedirà all'editore. Tra quindici giorni, tra un mese, potrà aver tra le mani il suo libro, accarezzarlo, sentirne il peso. Sulla copertina ci sarà stampato, oltre al titolo (che non è nemmeno un titolo: *Poesie*), un nome, e due date. (Come su una pietra tombale, gli vien fatto di pensare.) Le due date: 1910-1960—il nome: . . .

hope and wish for one more thing: that he can find
throughout the volume a single vein of thought and of
feeling: and a kind of tonal coherence or consistency: and a
stubborn striving toward a form of simple lines and
transparent meanings: in sum, the imprint of an individual.
Of one unpossessed by the frenzy of the new, who instead
is pleased to feel himself to be in the poetic tradition of his
own region, his own land; of one who believes, even in
these chaotic times, in the sacredness of beauty, just as his
master Petrarch believed in it (in times, for that matter, no
less chaotic than our own). So be it. I would only implore
the honest reader to begin reading my book in the third or
the second part. In that way he will find my earliest sins
less unjustifiable: *peccata iuventutis meae.*

With these or similar words, spoken silently to himself,
the old poet, sitting with his mound of galleys before him,
finds such comfort as he can, enough to finish his reading,
his laboring.

The galleys are all corrected. Tomorrow morning he
will send them to the publisher. In fifteen days, in a month,
he will hold his book in his hands, stroke it, feel its weight.
Printed on the jacket, in addition to the title (which is not
even a title: *Poems*), will be a name, and two dates. (As on a
tombstone, he begins to think.) The two dates: 1910-1960—
the name: . . .

Diego Valeri

The Lockert Library of Poetry in Translation

George Seferis: Collected Poems (1924-1955), translated, edited, and introduced by Edmund Keeley and Philip Sherrard

Collected Poems of Lucio Piccolo, translated and edited by Brian Swann and Ruth Feldman

C. P. Cavafy: Collected Poems, translated by Edmund Keeley and Philip Sherrard and edited by George Savadis

Benny Anderson: Selected Poems, translated by Alexander Taylor

Selected Poetry of Andrea Zanzotto, translated and edited by Ruth Feldman and Brian Swann

Poems of René Char, translated by Mary Ann Caws and Jonathan Griffin

Selected Poems of Tudor Arghezi, translated and edited by Michael Impey and Brian Swann

"The Survivor" and Other Poems by Tadeusz Różewicz, translated and introduced by Magnus J. Krynski and Robert A. Maguire

"Harsh World" and Other Poems by Ángel González, translated by Donald D. Walsh

Ritsos in Partheses, translations and introduction by Edmund Keeley

Salamander: Selected Poems of Robert Marteau, translated by Anne Winters

Angelos Sikelianos: Selected Poems, translated and introduced by Edmund Keeley and Philip Sherrard

Dante's "Rime," translated by Patrick S. Diehl

Selected Later Poems of Marie Luise Kaschnitz, translated by Lisel Mueller

Osip Mandelstram's "Stone," translated and introduced by Robert Tracy

The Dawn Is Always New: Selected Poetry of Rocco Scotellaro, translated by Ruth Feldman and Brian Swann

Sounds, Feelings, Thoughts: Seventy Poems by Wisława Szymborska, translated and introduced by Magnus J. Krynski and Robert A. Maguire

The Man I Pretend to Be: "The Colloquies" and Selected Poems of Guido Gozzano, translated and edited by Michael Palma, with an introductory essay by Eugenio Montale

D'Après Tout: Poems by Jean Follain, translated by Heather McHugh

Songs of Something Else: Selected Poems of Gunnar Ekelöf, **translated by Leonard Nathan and James Larson**

The Little Treasury of One Hundred People, One Poem Each, **compiled by Fijiwara No Sadaie and translated by Tom Galt**

The Ellipse: Selected Poems of Leonardo Sinsigalli, **translated by W. S. DiPiero**

The Difficult Days **by Robert Sosa, translated by Jim Lindsey**

Hymns and Fragments **by Friedrich Holderlin, translated and introduced by Richard Sieburth**

The Silence Afterwards: Selected Poems of Rolf Jacobson, **edited and translated by Roger Greenwald**

Rilke: Between Roots, **selected poems rendered from the German by Rika Lesser**

In the Storm of Roses: Selected Poems by Ingeborg Bachmann, **translated, edited, and introduced by Mark Anderson**

Birds and Other Relations: Selected Poetry of Dezsö Tandori, **translated by Bruce Berlind**

Brocade River Poems: Selected Works of the Tang Dynasty Courtesan Xue Tao, **translated and introduced by Jeanne Larsen**

The True Subject: Selected Poems of Faiz Ahmed Faiz, **translated by Naomi Lazard**

GPSR Authorized Representative: Easy Access System Europe - Mustamäe tee 50, 10621 Tallinn, Estonia, gpsr.requests@easproject.com

www.ingramcontent.com/pod-product-compliance
Lightning Source LLC
Chambersburg PA
CBHW051527230426
43668CB00012B/1767